llorando y

sonriendo

miranda morales espinosa

dedication ~

to those who feel too much, risk too
much, give too much, and love too
much... you are all valid

to everyone i left behind.

to everything that could have been.

para mi abuelita: te amo con todo mi
corazon y simepre estas en mi mente.
todo lo que hago es para irme a verte a ti
y toda mi familia.

to everyone i have met.

to everyone i have loved.

to everyone i love.

to everything that has happened and will
happen.

to the one person that has shown me
what true friendship is: ygml.

to the tiny victories that keep me going.

to myself: open your eyes to the what you've manifested. it's beyond what you've imagined.

contents:

introduction:

trusting in love. trusting with love. trusting in anything or anyone has always been one of the hardest concepts to grasp. for me. it will always be something foreign to my intuitive nature. slowly but surely i am thinking of trust more as a form of love rather than a tool or concept. for over three years i have been constantly reminding myself to breathe and trust in certain people. in certain situations. in life. in the universe. reminding myself that i cannot always have control over every little thing. i need to let things play out accordingly. there is one month left in the year, and i can finally physically see everything falling into place. everything that is meant for me is coming together. slowly but surely. i have also been reminding myself that i need to trust in the fact: nothing is forever. everything is temporary. people, situations, and state of minds are not eternal. love can be eternal, but not the people we love. physically speaking. we can always carry them in our hearts whether they're dead or alive. so even if everything is falling into place, it isn't forever. it is only for a time being. i'm trying to make peace with that, but like i said it is not in my intuitive nature. i want to believe that people will never fade from our lives. at least their memory will always last. at least a happy memory. at least the memory of being happy in their presence. at least the sense of happiness. do you know what i mean?

outrage

an open letter ~

remember: family is a simple complex root.
complex with all its baggage. simple with all its
love. love is greater than the complexity, so we
accept them all. different cultures. different
people. different traditions. the differences are
what makes it all beautiful beyond the
separations. beyond the crying children. beyond
the mothers and fathers mourning. beyond the
brokenhearted families who don't even know
where their own children are. that is what family
is. familia es una bella cosa pero when they
separate a child from their parent's arms and
home then it taints the root, but it will never
taint the love. it will never taint everything the
familia has built and lived for. those children
will one day rise to be the beautiful human
beings they already are. don't forget about them
because they are crying for freedom. children
are crying for freedom in their own country. not

for toys or materialistic things that don't matter. for freedom. can you hear them? please, tell me you can because their family is still searching for their cry, for their well-being, por su amor. please, listen because their strength is what is holding them together. they need their mami and papi's love. they need to know everything is going to be okay, but we cannot promise that unless we have people who are fighting for the freedom they cry for. please, help us help them. they just want to go home. home to their familia. home is where their family is, and home to them will always be united states of america. this is their home, so please help us help them to go home. they just want to go home. don't you feel their pain as they're crying for home. for their mamis and papis. for their hermanitas and hermanitos. for freedom.

outrage ~

reflecting to reset. broken hearted with
everything that's going on in our country,
world, and earth. turn on the news and inform
yourself. don't rely on one news source. don't
believe headlines. read the whole article. cross
reference it. do your own research. don't believe
everything you're told. don't trust anyone.
think, speak, and live for yourself. love who you
want to love. at the end of the day, love is all we
really have. if it makes you happy then hold
onto it for as long as you can. don't be fooled
with what you see on social media. people
project what they want you to believe. do your
research and trust the facts.

speak for the unspoken ~

even when the world brings us down, even
when our own country is under fire, even when
we are disgraced everyday by the most ignorant
president of all time: we will still stand with
each other. we will walk with love for one
another. we will march with our heads held up
high. our voices will not be silenced. we will be
heard loud and clear. we are women. we are
empowered and empowering. women are the
base of love. this love will flourish from the
earth's roots to the leaves on the highest trees.
it'll blossom and bloom until the whole world
can feel it. until, every person feels the nurturing
freedom in their soul. until then, we stand up
and fight for what's right. until then, i will
always speak for the unspoken.

it's so easy for the white man to say ignorance is bliss. reality is: ignorance is an idiotic state of stupidity.

black lives matter ~

black lives matter…black lives matter…black lives matter…for hundreds of years this unfair country has been a disgrace in the eyes of god when it comes to racial differences. ripped from their homeland…dragged to an unknown land and forced to call it home. spat on, treated like animals, murdered in cold blood because of the color of their skin, but we all bleed red. don't we? we are all the same, yet all the ignorant minds are too blind to see that…black lives matter…every single person is a human, no matter the color of their skin…so why is it that we differentiate black and white… or even color and white. all the agony and hate cannot be forgotten, for it will always be in the history of this country. what if god could speak to each and every one of us? yes, he loves all his children, but he can still be honest to tell us when we are in the wrong. a high number of people would be in the wrong for being racist, but that does not matter to them. in all reality, they are proud of themselves when chanting all lives matter…white lives matter…but black lives matter… for god's sake and the peace of this country, we must all unite and firmly stand together. no one can tear down a strong held union…everyone needs to hear the pain caused by the hatred of a skin color. everyone needs to hear the damage it has left in millions and millions of hearts because no one should be told what they can or cannot do solely because of the color of their skin. we must stand as one and chant…black lives matter…maybe then the ignorance will fade away. even if it does not, it should be silenced. for once, black lives should not be scared…for once, there should be harmony…for once white lives should chant black lives matter…for eternities black lives should be able to live without the fear of being murdered because of the color of their skin. and

one day the world will remember the harmony
between every race when all lives
chanted…black lives matter.

puzzle ~

lately i've been trying to be naive, i've been
trying to piece all of my hurt into this puzzle of
confusion. into this puzzle of mania. into this
puzzle called life and trying to figure out where
my piece fits. where i make sense in it all. i
guess i never really thought it would race
through my mind quite frequently than it
actually does. i want to believe i can make a
difference. i want to believe i was put into this
world to aid it so it can heal. i want to believe i
can do good on planet earth while i'm still
breathing. while i'm still able to run, dance, and
scream. scream for everyone who has ever been
oppressed by the white man. oppressed because
their dream was too pure for the cold hearts of
racists. i will never stop. i will never take a
break. i will always want to make racists afraid.

confiar con amor

reality check with self ~

it's so hard sometimes. i want to give up. i just
want to say: mom, dad... i tried my best. i'm
going to go back home because college is too
much for me. i miss being home. i miss being
able to wake up in my own bed. walking to their
room. massaging my mom's back. something as
simple as that. i miss them. i miss my dad
getting up earlier than all of us, and just waking
us up because he wants to spend time with us. i
miss sophia. i miss my sister. i miss her so
much. she's the best thing that could have
happened to me besides my parents. i miss
them, but i'm over here doing everything that i
can for them because they dreamed a better life
for me and sophia... and i don't want to screw
things up. i don't want to fail what they have in
mind for me, and i know what they have in
mind for me is what they want for me to have in
my mind for myself. they want me to dream for

myself, but in those dreams that they have for me; they want me to dream that i go to college and i get a degree and i get the career and i get the money and i'm able to live a better life they lived because they struggled. they struggled when they were young. they struggled in their wonder years. they struggled when they met. they struggled when they got married. they struggled when they had me. they're not struggling anymore, but they don't want me to experience the struggle they have lived through. and i don't know how i feel about that because i want to give them everything they never had, but i just don't know how i'm going to get it. i have to do it. there is no doubt about that. i'm going to pursue my dreams. i'm going to do everything in my bone and living humanly body to do everything they ever wanted. for them. with them. no matter what because i'm their daughter. i came from their blood. i came from their past. i came from their ancestors. my

ancestors. it's my blood. it's my past. it's my
future. it's their future. its everyone's future,
and i'm tired of thinking that i can't do it
because in reality i can do it. i am able to do it. i
have every single opportunity in front of me that
i can do it.

my horoscope told me today i was going to have
a conversation with someone who doesn't
understand what i am going through… but
maybe that person is myself. i need to
understand myself. i need to know that my
issues matter. and i need to know that i can go to
people whenever i need it. i just need to know. i
just need to let people know that i need them.
that i need them with me at times i don't feel
like myself. at times where i feel like the world
is crashing on me. at times when i feel like
dying. like the world is going to be fine without
me. i need to let people know because you never
know. anything can happen and everything will

happen. i don't want to die without anyone knowing how i truly felt and how i truly believed. and how i truly dreamed. and how i truly want to love and how i love and how i wish and how i hope and how i'm struggling. i want them to know they're not the only ones who struggle, but i need to let myself know that i'm not the only one struggling.

i have so many hopes and dreams that i want to keep living until i try my absolute best. and so many dreams that i have which i know what they are and maybe no one else does but i do. and i'm going to keep going until i can because that is who i am. that is who my parents raised me to be. that is who i am inspired by. that is who i will be.

all i know in this moment is that i'm going to be okay.

i love you, okay? i love you self. i love you. i love everything about you. just keep going.

you're doing wonderful. you're doing better than yesterday. you're doing better than last year. you're doing better than three years ago. than four years ago. than five years ago. you're doing so great. you're proving yourself wrong, proving everyone wrong who doubted. you're doing just fine. just prove yourself wrong. nobody else. you're doing just fine.

you'll be okay. you're more than fine. you're on this level that nobody can touch you. and if they try to touch you, they might succeed a little bit, but you will rise back up because that is what you do. you're the most resilient human being i have ever met. i'll catch up with you, self. tomorrow, next week, next year. in five years, ten, twenty, thirty years. you're going to take it day by day because that is how life works. you're going to live a beautiful life.

the only things that you need to take care of are the things you need to do today.

nothing is forever. everything is temporary, and
i am still trying to grasp that reality.

wonderfully gracious woman ~

i look at myself and what do i see? i see a girl
who became a woman with the sole purpose of
conquering her world. a woman who is still
trying to figure herself out. i am filled with
anxiety for the future. i am filled with anxiety
for the present. i am not filled with regret for my
past… for the past is the past. who am i? i am a
kind soul. i am a soul filled with love. i am a
wander lusting soul. i am many things and more.
i am so much more than a daughter, sister, and
friend. i am a woman.
i am a delicate woman who needs to be cared
for with delicate hands.
i am a headstrong woman who needs to be
challenged with different opinions.
i am a loving woman who loves every person
she opens her mind and heart to.
i am a woman who feels everything without
hindering any emotion from herself and others.

i am a woman who is terrified of dying loveless.
i am a woman who has the capacity to love a
million lifetimes.
i am a woman who wants to be loved by the
right person… even if it is at the wrong time.
i am a woman who adores people that don't
deserve my adoration.
i am a woman who opens her heart with open
arms to a man that disgraces the honor of being
loved by her.
i am a woman who will never give up on the
people she loves.
i am a woman with an open ocean mind who is
ready to accept the world.
i am a woman who wants to help the world.
i am a woman of color who is in love with her
brown skin.
i am an intelligent woman who does not let
weak minded men degrade or patronize her
because they feel threatened.
i am a creative woman.

i am a powerful woman… no, i am a fucking
powerful woman.

i am a woman who loves being adored.

i am a heavyhearted woman.

i am a lighthearted woman.

i am a woman who cries.

i am a woman who smiles.

i am a strong woman.

i am a weak woman.

i am an independent woman.

i am a dependent woman.

i am a confident woman.

i am a self-conscious woman.

i am a careless woman.

i am a woman who cares.

i am an empathetic woman.

i care too much.

i love too much.

i think too much.

i hold on too much.

i hold in too much.

i miss too much.

i let go too much.

i risk too much.

i am me. too much of the time, i think i am an imposter living in a wonderfully gracious woman's body…

but then i remember i am that woman. i am that wonderfully gracious woman. i am me. no one else can be me. i have to love myself enough to see the truth… and thank god, i do. i am a woman who does love herself. thank god.

sometimes you have to remind yourself that it only matters what you think about yourself. you are your own biggest and sometime only fan. treat yourself with the dedication, credit, and love you deserve.

burdened ~

burdened with the need of money for getting by. deprived of the one thing holding my sanity together. sleep. my family. my friends. love. i need love to get by. i need my family and friends to get by. but how is it where society dictates the one thing we need most is money. at the end of the day, money is not going to be there for me. money is not going to hold me while i cry. money is not going to tuck me into bed at night when the nightmares come back. you know sometimes i can't sleep. i can't sleep because the anxiety keeps me up. the anxiety of how my family is. how my friends are. how will it be when i grow up… when my responsibilities become more than me. they become the nightmares where i cannot make ends meet because my twenty-year-old self needed time. with family. with friends. with someone more than just herself. needed time to be loved and cared for instead of burdening her days and nights with work. not wanting to go to school because the creative in her just doesn't get why school should dictate what she wants to be when she grows up. i know what i want to be. i want to be so much more than the space i'm being held in. i want to be more than the standard i am held to. i want to write. i want to let my words flow onto a page for the rest of my life. i want writing to be more than my getaway. my cry for help. each time i reach out, i do it out of a cry for help. each time i reach out, it is killing me, and i don't know how much longer i can survive.

paving the way, so one day my sister, my
children, grandchildren, great grandchildren,
and so on will never feel the need to follow a
path that is not theirs. wanting them to feel the
freedom to do whatever the fuck they want in
life.

alternate reality ~

as i sit here in my dim room, i ponder of what my life would have been like in a different world. in reality, it is not a far distance from where i stand, but in all honesty it is far away…mentally. emotionally, i am there. mentally, it is an unknown world compared to what is known. as i stare at the screen, i ponder to what are their thoughts…towards me…towards their family…towards what i was then to what i am now. different perspectives create a spectrum of the world in a bird eye's view. as i toy with words in my gloomy room, i ponder if the spectrum has created an access to the minds of millions. in other words, compassion…empathy…understanding. it is not easy when every time contact is being made, it is from a device. especially when devices have ruined the lives of many. i am rambling and rambling…but that is only because it does not matter whether i can tell what my family is thinking or feeling. what matters and what is truly important is that i miss them. every single day of my life, i miss them. i ponder to what my life would have been like because at least i know in another world i would have had the opportunity to live amongst them. i would have had the opportunity to be what i am. a niece, a cousin…a granddaughter. i miss them, for they are a part of me. i miss them, for i will never know what my life would have been like with them… physically. all i can say now is, i look forward to the day where i can greet them with open arms, for that will be the happiest day of my life.

breathing in. taking a breath. trying to relax my ached muscles into a tranquility. releasing the pain and trying my best not to inhale it back in.

breathe with patience ~

they say patience is a virtue. my horoscope tells
me. my parents tell me. my friends tell me. my
best friend tells me. i tell myself. i just can't do
it. i don't have patience to wait. i'm impatient. i
want things right on the spot when i want them
because i know later on i will regret it. if i don't
want it later on then what's going to happen
when i actually have it. my heart is pounding
with something i want, but i don't necessarily
know if i can have it. is it love? is it lust? i'm
not sure, but all i know is i want to live now. i
want to enjoy life. i am impatient because i want
to know what life is about. i don't know what is
out there for me because sometimes i feel like
this country doesn't love me even when i want
it. even when i love it. sometimes i want to say
forget the past and let me look at the future.
patience is a virtue. i get it, but i don't want to
wait on something that may never happen. so

please god if you can hear me… if you're listening, please tell me what is there for me besides waiting. you have shown me so much already, but i can't seem to find it. blessings on blessings on blessings. i have the job. i have my family. i have friends. i have plans. this is what i wanted, but i still feel insecure about the future. i guess that's how it is. insecurity for the future will always come with anything and everything no matter what… breathe.

my heart hurts whenever i wake up from a
dream within a dream within a dream.
sometimes the inception is bittersweet. some of
the time it feels like a never-ending nightmare
devouring my mind, body, and soul.

mercury in retrograde note to self ~

how are you? i know you have been in a
whirlwind of emotions, but you have to take a
step back and realize how beautiful you have it
right now. don't push people away, but also take
some time to yourself... especially since there is
so much to process. it feels like a whole new life
all over again... but remember we went through
this over a year ago. a new life was upon us. a
new job, a newfound sense of freedom. a new
perspective on life. now look at you... it started
all over again with some bumps in the road. you
hate the job you loved a year ago. you distanced
yourself from the people who actually gave a
shit. even if you're trying to reconnect now it
won't be the same and who knows if it's for
better or worse. i guess you'll figure it out, but
trusting people is not your strong suit. trust
always has something to do with pushing people
away only to reel them back in. self, you have to

trust people in order to keep them in your life, through your ups and downs. you can't push people away when the depression creeps in. trust self to trust self. trust self to trust others. trust others to trust others. trust in one to trust in all.

i'm in a city where i don't belong

i'm in a city where i don't know where i'm from

i'm in a city where i want to spread my wings

i'm in a city where i don't know what that
means

take a minute and breathe. center yourself and
find your inner strength to love

lo siento ~

lo siento. i'm sorry mama. i'm sorry papa. lo
siento. i'm not your perfect mexican daughter.
everything you want from me, i can't give to
you. i'm at that age where i want to do todo lo
que quiero. everything that i want while still
living bajo de tu techo. under your roof. i want
to go out late at night and party with my friends.
after i want to come home and kiss you good
night. i want to follow my passion without
breaking your hearts. i want to get tattoos
without threats of being kicked out. i want to
love who i want to love without the fear of
being disowned. i don't want to be abandoned
by the only people i know as safety and love. i
want to be able to live my life without causing
you angustia. anguish. without causing you
sufrimiento. suffering. without feeling like i'm a
piece of shit for making you feel like i'm a
disappointment when in reality i'm not a

disappointment. i can live my life the way i want to, respectfully to you. because at the end of the day you are my mama and papa, but this is mi vida. my life. no tuya. not yours. you did bring me into this life raising me with loving arms and hearts. this life i'm living needs to be lived my way and my way only. lo siento. i'm sorry but i'm not your perfect mexican daughter. quiero hacer lo que me da la pinche gana. quiero seguir siendo tu hija. i want to do whatever the fuck i want while still being your daughter. while still having your love and admiration. while still having your support. i am still your daughter. i may not be perfect in a lot of ways, but i'm perfect in my ways. lo siento that it's not in the way you imagined me to be. i'm going to get a tattoo, and i'll still be someone in life. i'm going to follow my dreams. i'm going to marry whoever i want. i'm going to do lo que me da la pinche gana with or without your blessing. i just hope that you can still be by my

side mama y papá con amor. with love. because
no matter what, i will always have your back
while loving you every single minute of my life.
lo siento mamá y papá. i'm sorry mom and dad.
i'm not perfect.

doubt is poison to the mind. sometimes the only person who can save you from destruction is yourself… but doubt will always come raging with a fire for victory.

early bird ~

waking up early before everyone else. just to give myself a few moments to myself. □

hearing nothing, but the birds singing. seeing nothing, but the sun rising on my part of the east.

awake, breathing the cold crisp air. feeling the warmth of my toes. feeling the warmth of my momo against my toes.

trying to remember my dreams that seemed too real to be just a dream. trying to make sense of everything i just lived through in the past night. everything that ever was or is or will ever be in a dream.

remembering why i live unapologetically: i do what i want whenever i want. if someone has a problem with that then it's on them. believing in myself in what i do on a daily basis and long term is something i will never regret.

still her ~

still her. still me. still that girl you always
wanted me to be. still that girl i always wanted
to be. still blind as far as i can see. still drenched
in anxiety and doubt. for today. for tomorrow
and yesterday. still trying to figure it all out. still
have a plan. still have a vision. still have a
motive to do better. to be better. to try one last
time. still standing. here. there. still breathing.
deeply in. deeply out. still surviving. still living.
still trusting in love again. and again. and again.
still waiting for a tomorrow with you in it. still
waiting on a love that forgives and
wholeheartedly nurtures my broken soul. still
waiting for you. still waiting for you to be that
person. the person i thought you out to be. the
person you've always wanted to be. i guess that
changed. changed for you. changed for me.
changed for the reality of a lifetime far away.

has your heart ever hurt like you could feel your chest actually ache with this deep sadness? yes? me too. i feel it almost every day.

□□□□□□□□□□□□□□□

holding ~

believe in yourself enough to trust yourself to
hold yourself in whatever state you are in.

are you holding yourself how you should be?
with no expectations. endless love.
accountability. however and whatever state you
are in.

never think twice about loving deeply... never
doubt your chance to be deeply loved especially
by someone who has shown that they are
capable of holding you. however and whatever
state you are in.

purpose and meaning ~

the lovely unorthodox. what does it generally
mean? i am still figuring it out. what is it? a
universal place where love and compassion
flourish between the creases of my palms and
toes. what does it stand for? everything and
everyone.

after seven years, i am still establishing the
lovely unorthodox. it will always be in the
process of establishment because what it means
to me is myself. the journey in all aspects of my
life, especially love. love that was made from
scratch. an unwanted love that just wanted to be
embraced by self. self was lost and found, lost
and found, lost and found, repeating itself
repeatedly.

the love in its present time has been more than
just embraced. it has been planted with caressed

hands, watered with compassion, and shined on with grace. blooming with empathy.

here i am opening my arms to you, for you.

it is okay to cry in pain; it is okay to smile and laugh in bliss.

i am here.

i am here to wipe away your pain with mine.

i am here to laugh alongside of your laughter.

i am here as the lovely unorthodox.

the lovely unorthodox. a lovely woman who is unorthodox in every single way.

tune

tune in ~

as i close my eyes to rest, i picture us in another
lifetime dancing under my taurus moon. we're
grooving it out to a tune only you and i know; a
tune we created through moving our bodies as
one. a tune i remember, but one you forgot. we
said a prayer long ago; hoping we would find
each other again when our last breath left us; but
i guess we didn't want it enough because
decades later and i'm still here wide-eyed
waiting for a sign that you're out there. a sign
from the universe letting me know you're on
your way, but i'm still waiting. waiting is a
game i don't like to play, don't you remember? i
don't think so; your memory was always a little
faded. you always let things go without keeping
in mind you might need it later on. maybe my
words will find a way to you since i still
remember you... i still remember us. i remember
our intertwined hands creating a paved way for

each other. we would tell each other our dreams and fears. we would explore each other's mind with a single embrace. we were way more than lovers. do you remember me now? a lifetime ago, we built everything we had on our friendship. i'd help you reach the milky way, and you'd carry me to safety. i made sure you never gave up on your dreams, and you made sure i never gave up on myself. don't you remember our prayer? i do; i remember it all, but i don't remember your face. all i can recall is our love, and that's all i truly have to keep with me since no signs have come whether you are near or far. maybe you're right beside me, and i'm clueless to the fact. maybe i walked by you only to be lost in a crowd. maybe we will never find each other again. our paths never to intersect. it's not okay. i may have enough love left over to keep me company, but i'm still lost without you. i'm still wandering the streets waiting for someone to hold me until my aching heart can breathe again; but i don't let anyone near me because none of them feel like home; none of them are you. none of them know our tune.

some people don't understand that to receive

love you must give love.

look me in the eyes ~

look me in the eyes and confess to me all of
your sins. all the sins that caused me pain. every
single moment you carelessly danced while
making me desperately sing. look me in the eyes
and confess every single emotion you felt when
we were high on each other's presence. how just
being together in the same atmosphere made us
overlook our past and future. the present seemed
too sweet to the taste to ever believe there could
be another time where you and i would part
ways. look me in the eyes and confess your true
heart's desire. i know it is me. it has always
been me. right? after all, you were mine. i will
look into your eyes and relinquish the pain in
my chest. don't you know? my heart hurts…
even with just the thought of you. the memories
of you. i will break free from your embrace to
run into my own. my own embrace has a
warmth i have always missed. i will look into

your eyes and boil the tears with the fury in my lungs. my ancestors did not sacrifice everything for me to cry every single night about someone who is not worthy. i breathe their air, i breathe for everything i ever stood for. i will look into your eyes, only to look away into the eyes of my own reflection. i look into my eyes and i see an eternally powerful woman who will never allow herself to be under appreciated, disrespected, or taken for granted by a man who doesn't value himself enough to value her. there were more times than i would like to admit where i blamed my vulnerability for the fractures in cherished relationships, but i was never to blame. my eyes could never be the fault of another's inability to love me. i look into my eyes and i am in awe of the woman i am becoming. a dulce XXXexicana dipped in pure golden miel who is barely beginning to discover what she is capable of. you can look at me all you want… watching from a distance… contemplating with the wonder of the what if's and maybe's… staring hoping to catch my glance… the only difference between you and i is that i won't be looking back.

reminder: don't take for granted the ones who deeply love you. the ones who took care of you at your darkest of times. the ones who never forgot who you really are. the ones who carry your heart in theirs.

look at me now ~

look at me now with your tenderly sweet eyes,
do you see my soul?

will you accept my soul? i did not think so.

you are a beautiful human being, but i am a
majestic being from outer space.

the difference is that you are who you are, and i
am who i am with grace.

i do not mean outer differences, i mean inner
differences

you fall and expect me to be there for you, but
when you have risen you forget who helped you
in the darkness, for instance

but there are various instances where you've
shown me you are capable of loving me, and
other times where you are uncappable

so which is it my love? you are not mine, but i call you with a heart full of love and no, i do not fable

the truth is… i am nothing to you and you are everything to me

you are who you are, you feel what you feel

and i cannot change you… those were never my intentions

all i wanted was for you to love me with pure intentions

people come and go in life, but that doesn't
mean it's okay. it is what it is, and there's no
way you can change that. that's the reality of it
all.

lost letters ~

i haven't talked to you in years... like really talked about what's going on in your life, work, school, or through your head when life is up or down. but you showed up in a dream of mine. it was so realistic! you should've seen us! it was like the old days when we were little kids with no worries; but in the dream, we were adults figuring out what to do with our lives. the part i wish we had in reality (and maybe we have yet to experience) is that no matter what was going on we had each other to lean on. with love. with trust. with love. anyways... i'm rambling like i always do, but you already knew that about me. i want to hear about you. how's life? how are you as a person? how's your well-being? i hope you're doing more than well because you deserve that; and if i ever do cross your mind, i hope you have the courage to actually hit send because i definitely don't..

deeply love the ones who deeply love you

one of mine ~

they give me hope. i thought i was lost and
broken; but every time we look in each other's
eyes, all i am able to feel is how everything is
going to be okay. i used to think and believe my
world was ending; but in the end, i was always
going to persevere. i have to keep reminding
myself i am stronger than i claim to be. i'm
more than what i make myself out to be. i am a
valuable and lovable human being. yes, i loved
and lost... but i found love again. not only in
myself, but with them as well. they may not
know my love yet, but i know theirs. i may be
wrong, for they have been aware of my love all
along and to how much it can grow. if this is the
way to go then i thank the universe for crossing
our paths. if we must go our separate ways then
i'm still able to call them a blessing instead of a
lesson, for not all people are meant to stay in
your life regardless of who they are or what they

signify. we have multiple soulmates in our lifetime, i'm just at peace that they're one of mine.

triggered ~

i'm tired of pretending, and this whole
perception we have on each other. i've been
direct, why can't you? why can't you be direct
about what you want and don't want? i won't
get mad or offended. i just need to know. am i
wasting my time? or are you for real? is this a
temporary deal? or are you a soulmate? you see,
i want to love you... not this modern day love
where two people conditionally love each other
until someone "better" comes along. nahh, i
want to genuinely love you. where while the
whole world is in flames, we're laughing on a
high only we understand. i know that you know,
we go together like complementary colors.
while one shines, the other is illuminating in its
own right. i guess what i'm trying to tell you is
to let me know what you're feeling before i fall
in too deep...

surviving ~

when we think about past lives and lost loves,
are we really longing for the eternity of what
once was. or are we just longing the need to feel
something bigger than us as individuals. when i
think of a lost love, i do get a little sad
sometimes. i dig myself into a hole of sadness…
but i have to keep reminding myself every
second that they're gone that i am here standing
on my own two feet surviving and living on my
own.

letters to a fuckboy part one ~

my heart is racing. my heart is pounding. i don't
know what to do. i'm not sure if i should leap in
the air and say thank you god or if this is just
another thing the universe is trying to tell me
not to do because life would be better if i don't
do what i'm not supposed to do. that he may be
a really good dude. and maybe he is. but in this
moment he's not. i let him go. i said goodbye.
but i don't know if he'll… maybe it's not him.
maybe it's how he puts the words into play. the
way he said he loves my passion, but he never
really experienced my passion to know what my
passion is and what it feels like to be loved by
me. because in all reality, yes i did like him, but
i never loved him. see to be loved by me, he
would have never left me. to feel my love in
person, that constant love. he won't turn back.
he won't say goodbye. he'll just stay with me
forever and ever and i'll keep him close in my

heart and hug him and love him until we're together forever baby boy. it's just him and i until the end of time right? but no, it's okay though. i got used to the fact that people come and go; people come and go to the point where i'm like "it's okay because i'm used to it. i'm used to people leaving me. i'm used to people walking on their own away from me, to me. away from me. to me. away from me. to me. it's just a constant routine. see, i'm about to open a message because i literally told him straight up, "you're not down because you don't love me. you just say that to get to me." and right now he's going to say some stupid shit and i will read it because honestly let's see what he has to say.

see, this is a constant thing i keep telling myself: i'll never find anybody else because this is the only person who will ever give me butterflies and the sense that i can't breathe. i can't feel my knees. my knees are weak. literally. i walk to his door with my knees trembling. knowing that he might be the one for me, but i'm not sure because he talks in a misogynistic way that does not make me feel loved. it makes me feel like i'm his servant. it makes me feel that he's just using me. short term. but i'm not sorry. i was not put on this earth to please him. i was not made to please anyone but myself because that is who i am. i don't even please myself sometimes so why would he expect me to please him when he doesn't even know who the fuck i am.

confiando con amor es difícil cuando todos
te dan razones para que no confíes en nadie.

out of tune ~

i honestly thought i had everything figured out.
with love. with soul. with love. with soulmates.
it's not the first time i bite my tongue until i
taste the rich iron of blood. i should've known.
should've had an idea. it should've been fucking
obvious. you were always my first choice... i
would just press pause. because life. because
time didn't seem right. because your eyes
weren't set upon me. but could it be. or maybe
i'm delusional with a full taurus moon above us
in a clear midnight sky. my taurus moon. the
same one from long ago. could you be the
person who shares a tune so sweet with
familiarity? do you remember? i'm sorry i
confused other people to be someone they
weren't. maybe deep down you were always the
one who danced and sang to me as my head laid
on your chest. i just couldn't come to believe it
since the past of a current life masked who you

truly were. everyone who came across with a similar tune could not have been you. my eyes were cleared with truth to see the reality of their purpose. in my life. my purpose. in their life. both purposes were only temporary. as everything in life usually is. nothing is forever. everything is temporary, and i am still trying to grasp that reality. i don't want to grasp the reality that you might be another familiar tune... but i have to. you could be everything i have been waiting for... but i also don't want to get ahead of myself. at the same time, this current life has shown me who you could be or couldn't be. did you know you were in my dreams? each dream you would show up so vividly that i couldn't stop thinking about you the next following day. i felt as if you were so close but you were never actually there. in dreams. in life. in spirit. did you know i have written about you? lost letters only appeared to be a hidden manifestation. a manifestation that feels too close to be perfection in its present state. a manifestation that seems so easily self-sabotaged. by myself. not your doing. just mine. i do not want to repeat my mistakes. your mistakes. our mistakes. our parent's mistakes. everyone's mistakes. i do not want to let this go. it is something i keep struggling with. but you could be different. or you could be the same type of person with a similar purpose. or a different purpose. only time will tell. patience is virtue, but it is also a hell that makes my chest burn with a fire of doubts and hope. you give me hope. i give myself doubt. my fault. not yours. none of the time we spent apart is invalid but talking to you makes me wish we never lost communication. your laugh fills my heart with a warmth only home could give. only you could give. god damn... i really hope.. i'm praying the tune i grooved to some lifetimes ago was with you. i'm praying because i know it is you. you are my tune.

ojitos de miel ~

ojitos de miel // ¿me extrañas cómo te extraño a ti? no se por que pregunto... por que yo se la verdad. que ni piensas en mi... ni aparezco en tus sueños. está bien. i'll get over it.

tequila delusion ~

i get that he wasn't the one for me and maybe i'm just faded on some tequila. i'm honestly gone. i'm taking off my makeup, and i realize i just really wanted to make it work with one person in my life. why is it so hard to make it work, but then i realize to make it work with someone it means they need to be trying too. they have to be in it for the long run because if someone is in the short run with you, it's not going to work. you don't know what to do exactly because you've already given them so much of your life, and you just want to know is it okay? is it worth it even if i still walk away? but i get it. i know that one day i'll meet somebody, whoever it may be will treat me right and the way i want to be treated. and i hope when that day comes, i will embrace every little thing with open arms. and i don't close off my arms because once i ignore people it just seems to fade away. because i know once i start ignoring and ghosting they'll be gone and that's it until the next person that cherishes me comes along. one day my person will come to me. one day our paths will cross for the first time. and i'll be the happiest person in the world. but for now, i just feel hurt and that's okay to feel hurt because that is what i'm feeling right now. maybe one day but not today.

letters to a fuckboy part two ~

you're not a godly man. you say you love god.
that god is everything but god… god wouldn't
let you treat me like this.. god does not want you
to undermine me. to make me feel so degraded
that i'm sick to my stomach to the point where i
don't want to see anybody. i don't want to talk
to anybody. you don't love god the way you say
you do because if you did, you'd know how to
treat me right. you'd know how to treat women
right. you'd know how to treat people right. but
it's unfair to the fact that your ignorance has
you in a blissful melody. in all reality, you are
not a godly man. jesus christ or whatever. you
want to love jesus and god, but let me tell you
something: i do love god… and god i believe
she is a woman. she always appears as a woman
to me. i cry and cry internal tears because this is
not the way i should be treated this is not the

way anyone, any woman, any man, should be treated. you are not a godly man.

some may think i'm naive, but i like to put my bet on the chance that instead i'm filled with an intense hope... filled with a deep love which makes me willing to believe there is love out there. a real love. none of this short term, half effort, see you never kind of lust disguised as tainted love. there is a person out there who is meant for me, long term... and i am meant for them, long term.

333 ~

i was stuck in my head for a bit... everything was coming together all at once and i didn't know how to function.... the way your eyes look at me with tenderness and a side of lust made me forget the noise in my mind. for a minute, i had a bit of doubt buttt then i glanced away to clear my head and there it was. the communion of the confirmation. 333 staring me dead in the eyes. 333 blessing me with assurance of you. with you. i knew at that moment we were meant to be. in the moment. in that moment, i knew this was everything i have been waiting for. you are everything i have been waiting for. patiently. impatiently. now here you are with open arms and an open heart. i'm ready to receive you. i'm ready to drown myself in you. love you with everything i have in me. keeping your heart close to mine. making sure you never go a day with a doubt for my love. for my heart to yours.

for my intentions. for everything you mean to me. i'm ready. i'm ready to love you. i'm ready to take the necessary steps to make this last. i'm ready for the honeymoon phase and what comes after. i'm ready to take on this life with you. i'm ready.

coldness running through my veins. filling
each crevice it encounters forcing itself into
a hole where you used to call home.

funny ~

funny… funny how in middle school i was the geek. i was the nerd. the girl who wasn't all that pretty, but deep down inside of me i wanted to be. and i believed them. i believed the people, my friends, my school mates. i just believed i wasn't pretty. funny, still i had boyfriends in middle school or what middle schoolers call boyfriends. funny how in high school it didn't really go well for me in the dating world, but i didn't care. funny, how the same people who told me, told the world that they didn't think i'm pretty or would date me… are paying attention to me now as i am rising, as i am glowing to who i am supposed to be. and it's just funny how they would give me shit, but now they just want to praise me. funny how life works. funny how people want you at your highest, but don't want to be near you when you're at your lowest.

take care ~

sadness is deepening. world is crashing. heart is
crushed. lungs collapsed. swollen eyes filled
with tears. i can barely breathe. suffocation
takes over. bones and limbs weakening. curling
up into a pit of despair. soul vanishing.
memories tainted with pain. love will never be
the same. is this heartbreak? i never really knew
what heartache actually was until now, and it is
a fiery hell. i miss you. it's been a week since i
have kissed your lips. it feels like an eternity.
your lips on my lips is a heaven i can't portray
into words. your hand in mine is a home i want
to come back to. you are my home. not a
temporary one. you are my forever home even if
we never see each other again. i will always
want to come back to you. will you let me back
in when you're ready? ready to love. ready to
open your heart to mine. for now, i need to learn
how to breathe without my lungs collapsing into

a swallowing pit of self-loathing depression. i miss you, but i hope you don't miss me too much. i want you to live your life without anything holding you back. i do not want to be the one holding you back. be free my love. fly into the sky with your smile facing the stars. fly without a care in the world. i hope a lot and i just really hope one day you can fly back into my arms. i don't want to wait, but the reality is that i will. you are my forever. you are the love of my life. you are everything i dreamed about. you are everything i will ever want. you are my person. i miss you. i love you. i love you. i love you. please be good to yourself.

an unspoken conversation ~

- what do you want from me?

i want you.

i want you to look me in the eyes the same way i
look at you.

i want you to love me.

i want you to wrap your arms around me while
telling me everything will be alright.

i want you and only you.

can't you see that?

can't you see that you're all i ever wanted?

are you blind to my love for you?

i'm not trapping you.

i'm not holding you hostage.

i just want you to know that i love you so much, and that you're the one for me.

i'll never find someone like you.

i'll never feel the way i do about you with someone else.

unconditionally and whole heartedly, i'm here. for an eternity plus a lifetime....

- i'm sorry but i don't feel the same way. i hope you find your happy ending.

ajs ~

people talk, people sing, people love to yell and
scream, but do people love the way they should.
the way they want to. the way they need to. the
way their heart aches longing for one another.
for themselves. don't they know that their arms
want to be wrapped around their own warm
body. hold themselves so tight until they can't
ignore their own love. until their veins pump
and bleed. until the tears streaming down their
face make sense. until the pain in their chest
makes sense. until that pain goes away. don't
they know... don't they care... don't they know
that everything will come apart if they walk
away. from themselves. from the one person
they truly love. from everything they've ever
known as love. maybe it's better that way.
maybe it's better to walk away from a love that
can't be or won't be fed. from a love that only
knows the nurture from one but not the other.

does the other know the love that they seek is behind their shoulder. the love they offer can grow into a garden full of roses and trees... fruits and berries... not just the lonely flower in an empty pot. don't people like them know that love is what they need. from themselves. from you. from me. from everyone they seek. don't they know that love is really all anyone needs. but don't they just love to throw their arms in the air until the universe can hear their yelling and screaming. damning the world. asking how and why. don't they just love blaming the world for their tragedy. don't they just love spewing hate. don't they see what's right in front of them. a mind and mouth to feed. someone who will forever love them unconditionally and whole heartedly. someone. that someone hugs themselves so tight until they fall asleep wishing their arms were yours. loving themselves so hard so you won't have to love them back even when they love you unconditionally and whole heartedly. loving everything and everyone so that when you come back there will be no denial to your eyes of who they birthed themselves to be. a mother.. a nurturer for themselves... for you... for anyone they seek. don't you see. you can't see. no one will ever see. of who truly loves them when everyone falls asleep. when everyone is dreaming of the what if's, could have beens, and maybes. they'll be staring at the star filled sky hoping and praying you're alive with a well-fed mind and heart. hoping and praying that wherever you end up love is with you, love is held, love is remembered, love is love with a selfish wish that you remember them with love. with pride held aside. you remember them when love could still be young and reckless. when all that mattered was sitting side by side in the dead of night speeding through a city while stealing kisses at red lights and laughing the pain away. that will always be remembered. that will always be what matters.

that will always be remembered as love. don't they know...

fuck all of this no love shit. screw your praise
on yourself for being numb. i feel what i feel.
and i will never be ashamed for feeling love
intensely.

ajs farewell ~

it's not hard to believe because it's the reality of
what happened and what is.

i will never stop writing about you.

your fingertips left an imprint on my heart in a
way no one else could.

your fingerprints will never fade away.

your fingerprints will always hold my heart with
warmth.

i will never think of you with hate. with distrust.
with regret. with doubt. i will always think of
you with love. with hope. with trust.

trusting in the fact that you are who you are and
hoping wherever you are, you are happy with
love. in love.

we've gone our separate ways, but this will always be what i want for you. to be happy. in love with love. wherever love takes you i hope it carries you well. wherever love takes you, i hope it carries you back home. not to me, not to anyone else but yourself. wherever love takes you. whoever love is for you. i hope love carries you home.

final melody ~

drowning myself in pink floyd's melodies while trying to recover my sanity. knowing it'll all turn out to how it's supposed to, but still trying to understand that soulmates aren't meant to be in your life for forever. reminding myself that we'll meet again whenever the universe decides it's best. but who decided that the universe decides for us? at the end of the day, it's not up to me. it's not up to you, but i'll see you soon. i'm in no rush. let it be a year or a few because the next lifetime is an unbearable wait. shiiiiit.... i'm not mad or sad... definitely not happy at the moment but it still hurts. it hurt before. it hurts now and it will continue to hurt until we groove to our tune again. you are my tune. you have always been my tune. i just didn't know it until i met you. i've always known your melody without a face. the moment we met i knew you had a familiar face. the moment our lips met i realized who you are. you are my real soulmate. you are the muse that wakes me up at night to write countless verses and scriptures. you are more than who god had ever planned for me because you're home to me. i may not be home to you but that's okay. i have known from the start that my heart is meant to be a home. it's meant to carry with safety and love. nothing less. nothing more. it's unconditional. it's here to hold you without ownership or oppression. it's here if you ever need it. i'm here if you ever need me. can you hear me? are you listening? i'm here if you ever need me.

70419025R00061